GW01337151

# Poetry
## INTRODUCTION 2

# POETRY

## INTRODUCTION 2

FABER AND FABER
3 Queen Square
London

*First published in 1972
by Faber and Faber Limited
3 Queen Square London WC1
Printed in Great Britain by
Latimer Trend & Co Ltd Plymouth
All rights reserved*

*ISBN 0 571 09789 8 (hard bound edition)
ISBN 0 571 09790 1 (paper bound edition)*

*© This anthology
Faber and Faber 1972*

# CONTENTS

*Publisher's Note* *page* 11

## DICK DAVIS

| | |
|---|---:|
| Fish Tank | 15 |
| Jack the Giant Killer, grown old | 16 |
| A Mycenaean Brooch | 17 |
| The Diver | 17 |
| Rumours concerning a shopkeeper | 18 |
| Odysseus in Ithaca | 19 |
| Sleep | 20 |
| Her Going | 21 |
| Columbus to any court | 21 |
| Staying in one place | 22 |
| Youth of Telemachus | 23 |
| The Socratic Traveller | 23 |

## GREVEL LINDOP

| | |
|---|---:|
| Ovid in Exile | 27 |
| In a Footnote | 27 |
| The Place | 28 |
| Perplexed by the Sunlight | 29 |
| A Falling House | 30 |
| Too Much Care | 31 |

| | |
|---|---:|
| The Truth about Ariadne | *page* 31 |
| A Letter from Provence | 32 |
| Dream Image 3: Philosopher | 33 |
| The Messenger | 33 |

## ALASDAIR MACLEAN

| | |
|---|---:|
| Sea and Sky | 37 |
| Rams | 37 |
| Death of an Old Woman | 39 |
| At the Peats | 39 |
| The Beach in Winter | 40 |
| Snaring Rabbits | 41 |
| Horizons | 42 |
| Tallyman | 42 |
| Three-legged Frog | 43 |
| Fishing | 44 |
| Among Ourselves | 45 |
| Death of a Hind | 45 |
| The Old Dog | 46 |

## WES MAGEE

| | |
|---|---:|
| Maybe I'd do Well in Tibet | 49 |
| 'Sunday Morning' | 50 |
| The Holiday, and After | 50 |
| The Radish | 51 |
| Today's Lesson: an Observation | 52 |
| Happening | 54 |
| Postcard from a Long Way Off | 55 |
| Junior Junkies | 56 |
| Knowing | 57 |
| The Name Game | 58 |

PETE MORGAN

    Disguise    *page* 61
    The White Stallion    62
    The Red Monkey Poems    64
    The Rainbow Knight's Confession    66
    One of them was washing '*His*' body in Milk    68
    Pierre the Fibster Lives    69
    Wall    69
    & the Grey Mare being the better Steed    70

PAUL MULDOON

    The Inheritors    73
    Stillborn    74
    Unborn    74
    Skeffington's Daughter    75
    Snail    76
    Hedgehog    76
    The Indians On Alcatraz    77
    Poem for Lawrence    78
    Wind and Tree    79
    The Charcoal Burner    79
    Marble Orchard    80
    Aubade    81
    Hedges in Winter    82
    The Electric Orchard    82

WILLIAM PESKETT

    simile: you are    87
    The question of time    87
    Guns    88

| | |
|---|---|
| Impressionist Landscape | *page* 89 |
| Plants | 89 |
| rainbow | 90 |
| exodus | 91 |
| crayfish facts 1–4 | 92 |
| soldier | 92 |
| I'll watch my friend, the moving mountain | 92 |
| Dead man in a sunset | 93 |
| sandscape | 93 |
| Moths | 95 |
| Why I am the Last of the World's Great Lovers | 95 |
| Crom—April 1969 | 96 |

### RICHARD RYAN

| | |
|---|---|
| Knockmany | 99 |
| The Thrush's Nest | 100 |
| A Heap of Stones | 101 |
| Viking Deposits | 102 |
| Function | 104 |
| Moher | 105 |
| From My Lai the Thunder went west | 105 |
| Galaxy | 107 |
| Ireland | 108 |

### CLIVE WILMER

| | |
|---|---|
| Elegy for Donald Campbell | 111 |
| The Exile | 111 |
| The Goldsmith | 112 |
| Arthur Dead | 113 |
| Octogenarian | 113 |
| The Stone Circle | 114 |

| | |
|---|---:|
| Victorian Gothic | *page* 115 |
| The Well | 116 |
| Ghost King | 117 |
| | |
| *Biographical Notes* | 121 |

# PUBLISHER'S NOTE

In the *Introduction* poetry anthologies we aim to publish poets whose work has hitherto been available only in magazines or booklets with a very limited circulation, thus giving them the opportunity of making their first appearance before the general public. The number of contributors is small, which means that we have been able to publish a representative selection of work from them all. Each of the nine poets has his own individual voice, but we feel that they all share consistent qualities of intelligence and perception.

The poets included are Dick Davis, Grevel Lindop, Alasdair Maclean, Wes Magee, Pete Morgan, Paul Muldoon, William Peskett, Richard Ryan and Clive Wilmer.

# DICK DAVIS

## Fish Tank

His lover's room is high above the sea
Exposed to wind and every noisy storm
That soaks her window with congealing spray;
To him she says that only bed is warm——

From where, beyond her hand and dreaming face,
He sees the fish tank in the corner:
Gaudy, purposive, the gentle tropic fish
Turn slowly in their heated water.

Warm behind glass their garish colours gleam
And deliquesce: fronds braid a green obscurity
And killer fish pass silently between:
Electric lights illuminate their prey.

They lie together and silently he watches:
She drowses warm against his conscious flesh,
Brown hair unravelled on the pillow catches
Dim flickerings from the tank. His eyes adore the fish.

She leans to him and whispers, 'Do you love
Me?' His eyes feed on their pure unhindered
Poise—too slow, too sure for words they move,
Close on each meal. She does not catch his answer.

## Jack the Giant Killer, grown old

The iron scholars of the blood
Forget volition in a maze
Of reasons; where once the sword
Blazed through all intricacies
The hand lies numbed and dazed.

I clambered up the fabled stalk
And burned to face them man to man—
Now my purposes are dead—they walked
And blotted out the sun,
And so I lopped them, one by one.

My sword's length measured out their fall,
Their guts are now a stain, no more;
The sentinels gave way, each castle wall
Was crumbled at my touch; their whores
Betrayed them to my hands, my law.

But my task survives undone;
The broad land in the sky gapes empty,
But the stalk still reaches down
And binds its roots in spite of me:

Old now, I need hostility.

## A Mycenaean Brooch

Peace came back slowly, sealed
In iron, to which there
Is no answer. Wounds healed,

But silence guards Mycenae
Where I beat out useless
Bronze to fend off history.

From our last swords' broken
Blades I made my wife this
Brooch, survivor's token

Of her fathers' armour—
Though bronze will not protect
And may endanger her.

We shall leave for Ionia:
There islands may exist,
Too small for them, or far.


## The Diver

The blue-cold spasm passes,
And he's broken in.
Assailed by silence he descends
Lost suddenly

To air and sunburned friends,
And wholly underwater now
He plies his strength against
The element that

Slows all probings to their feint.
Still down, till losing
Light he drifts to the wealthy wreck
And its shade-mariners

Who flit about a fractured deck
That holds old purposes
In darkness. He hesitates, then
Wreathes his body in.


## *Rumours concerning a shopkeeper*

It was the tedium
Of his certainty
That gave his days
Their weightless currency.

He knew the time the
Doctor gave—and they
Did not who wondered
'Where his interests lay',

And thought perhaps
His force was burned
In furtive sex, or politics.
Now they have learned.

For when, one unespecial winter night,
He met his certainty,
He sold his tedium for nothingness
Quite willingly.

## Odysseus in Ithaca

He sits as if of stone;
At rest in the alien land,
 Unconscious of the sun,
The saltless water by his hand—

 His closed eyes lose the dream
He will not labour to retain,
 The swords more faintly gleam,
Night falls on Troy's dismembered plain;

 And equally he knows
He can no more rehearse the names
 Of those lost heroes whose
Dim shades the underworld now claims.

 He acts in fantasy,
Remote and satisfied, the tryst
 With glad Penelope.
He rises, and, as through a mist

 Of age and wars, he sees
His father's house, the heritage.
 Approaching it he hears
An unfamiliar noise. Cold rage

And cunning come to him
As if he stood again at Troy:
   He fills the doorway, grim
With loathing: they turn, and like a boy

   He smiles, and points to where
The huge bow hangs. His eyes are lit
   With an accustomed fire;
Shy as a slave he proffers it.


## *Sleep*

The body forces wings
Or falls. The angel with a levelled sword
Is sex and history
The darkness where you plummet, soar—

An emptied word
In rage for God. The trapdoor
Opens into
Nightmare limitless and wholly void.

You may do nothing here
By will but clamour for the unreal dawn.
It comes as fiction, a
Nostalgia: guilty, half-forgotten.

## *Her Going*

A person can create a place
That with her moving dies—
An absence of the special face
That held reality to be
A surface for the eyes
Can mean you cannot see.

And worse this absence can undo
Distinctions you have built
Between what is and what is you—
Until the corners ache with guilt
And rooms become the blind
Accomplices to break your mind.

## *Columbus to any court*

Not compulsion rives me thus
Into the sea, nor the hope of gain—

Distance must be ignored or traversed,
Irony's not easy for a sailing man.

My lords, I cannot beg, not even
Comprehension—and I am not assured

Or lucky, knowing only that
Contemplation without action is absurd.

My lords, I crave a ship for working in
And what's worked out if anything
Is all unknown:
    My lords, your pardon;
Your silence tells me more than words.

May the sun shine on your lasting houses,
May ease enfold your certain dynasties.

## *Staying in one place*

Staying in one place you stay to see
The landscape fade,
Slow rot invade
Each sentimental trysting tree.

Staying in one place the crusts wear thin,
The psychic mountains
Pare to sand grains,
And waters past the dykes flow in.

Staying in one place the patterns you
Thought perfect tangle,
The loose ends dangle
Wondering what, so late, there's still to do—

Until you grasp what seems your only chance,
Choose place and stance
And move (you say advance)
Toward new semblances of permanence.

## Youth of Telemachus

It is a land he knows. White sunlight
Specifies each shrub and stone—
And as he moves his vacant sight
Restores him to the ways he's grown:

He is enclosed in reveries
No will can break, and where he goes
A child's unfinished fantasies
Dictate the paths that he will choose.

He rises in the dawn: the sun
Illuminates where he will pause
And where proceed: at his return
He sleeps and dreams his father's wars:

Until one evening he delays,
Past sunset, sunk in memory:
He sees the moon rise and he stays:
All night he views the changing sea.


## The Socratic Traveller

Beneath the inconsistent skies
He moves, in sun and sudden rain,
The rinsed air following, his eyes
Undaunted, as if unaware
Of what might turn aside their stare
And mitigate the real terrain.

He begs the truth of all he sees—
The city and the village, plain
And moorland stream, the crowded trees,
Each street, each desolate high hill—
He finds no meaning but he will
Not mitigate the real terrain:

He prosecutes his pilgrimage
Toward the sceptic's partial gain
Of seeing what is false—the gauge
Of truth becomes whatever he
Cannot discern as sophistry
That mitigates the real terrain.

Until he penetrates by slow
Degrees to ignorance, the vain
Obverse of all that he would know:
And, pausing, he is made aware
It is his constant presence there
That mitigates the real terrain.

# GREVEL LINDOP

## Ovid in Exile

At the outposts of a broken language
I have lived lately. These barbaric provinces:
the worst wine in the empire, no books, and the most
execrable climate. (I have a few notes of
such grammar as persists here, having to instruct
my servants. His Imperial Highness would not
be interested.) A poem will not suffice
for this bone-grasping cold, let alone
death, or loneliness. Like the provincials,
such things would need physical violence
to make them intelligible. The grunts
of these oxen express them more accurately.

As for you, Julia, if you expect a poem,
you can go to the emperor and let him
fondle you with his greasy hexameters.

More real than any poem I can make
are the dreams of you that shake me
nightly, and wring me dry, body and mind.

And these I cannot send you, my dearest.


## In a Footnote

Let them mention in the biographies
the incident, shortly before
the start of his 'Major Period':

how they met (a mutual friend. . .)
the acquaintance, the friendship,
the (on his side) love.

He so sensitive, she
perhaps a bit overawed.
And when he dared to tell her,
her confusion, her silence
at the responsibility.

As for him, he knew
'when he was not wanted'. No-one
'was going to deny him a second time'.

And then the ticket to Paris,
the first of the great novels,
universal sympathy for him,
universal reproach for her.
Let them mention it, let them
sympathize once more.

And let them add in a footnote,
she loved him.


## *The Place*


There was a meeting: sometime. But the place
remains, for them, the constant. The dry
fountain and its dusty stone throat;
the point where buses stopped, anticipating
olive-traders from the market; the cafe.

Before this place came a chance encounter,
after it refuge in the hotel; a
delayed embrace; the solitude of dressing;
making the bed together, silent. All
less sharp, now, than the lemon sunlight
of the place caught in that marble cup
and remembered; or, perhaps, imagined.


## *Perplexed by the Sunlight*


The boy is perplexed by the sunlight:
after four days of sheltering
underground, outside the village,
he wanders homeward, to meet
chaos: the dead cattle, voices chattering,
the first fires being relit after the barrage.

Turning slowly above the delta,
the pilot edges over the green map
his silver triangle. Perplexed by the sunlight,
he only half-attends to the navigator,
is half-suprised to feel the cargo drop
and plane leap sunward; he cannot see the target.

# *A Falling House*

I have wandered all night long
through the great chaotic house
and pushed my way through the throng
of terrible strangers, their words
the more chilling because the sense
lies, always, just out of reach:

a deranged nobleman, cobweb-fingered
among his heavy-jewelled rings:
a psychopathic boy, who left
a dead child at the stair-foot:
a nurse fainted at the sight;
old men, friendly, coaxing as reptiles;
old women, lewd as toothless whores.

All night I fought my way
through the fetid vacuum of these other
selves, and today I see
how nearly I am of their kind:
and know that one day, one of them
may come to sit in the chair of my mind.

## Too Much Care

Able, in writing, to revise
any mistaken word or clumsy phrase,
we start to think: how much better
to write, than to meet face to face.
So writing becomes a shield; that is, a barrier.

Unable, in speech, to alter
things once said, we play for safety
now, say only what will bear repeating
and so shut out our hope of meaning—
the truth of gesture or emotion
too much care takes out, and can't replace.


## The Truth about Ariadne

No wonder Theseus fled the island,
leaving her there to die upon the sand,
her body torn by his child's life:
how else could he have exorcised the memory
of her dark face, and those small hands
holding the twine to thread the labyrinth?

And turning his love to shame, in his heart
remained the memory that after fighting
his way to the central chamber of the maze,
he found her there, laughing in triumph, proud
mistress of one spell no man's mind can break.

And so he raised a black sail for Aegeus,
took his revenge on woman-kind,
(Helen, Persephone, the Amazons)
trapped in anger against their timeless strength,
and saw in each what he most feared to see:
the mocking face of his wild-haired Ariadne—
whilst she, on Naxos, lay with Dionysus.


## *A Letter from Provence*

Certainly, she has style.
From the envelope, I shake out
a whole village: pink walls
spill together, the mountains settle
on my table, cypress-trees
straighten themselves among the clutter.

The church bell has a gummed back,
the main square is adorned
with a statue of France
cut from a postage-stamp.

But still those words are missing, love
may be there or may not.
The village waits, indifferent,
to be folded, and I notice
it is on paper, catches no light,
no shadows either of sun or moon.

So what? Folded, it looks smug;
has served, I suppose, her purpose.
Only a fool would tear it up.

## Dream Image 3

*Philosopher*

>Restless in the evening,
>he took paper boats
>and set them sailing
>from the shore of his thoughts,
>watching them a little after
>they passed out of sight.

## The Messenger

The poet stayed two days
longer than the rest
under the volcano: there were books to be sorted,
a pile of manuscripts to move
(last corrections, supplements
to poems sent out before).
The house and garden rang
in the morning with bewildered quietness
all children being at a distance,
only an occasional hungry dog
that yawned and snapped, restless,
and ate the scraps he left it.
The telephone disconnected, he
(sleeping five hours of the night)
watched the red glow rising and
typed, annotated, drank.

On the third day, bottle
in hand, he left the door
to bang in the wind (the only door in town
unlocked) and headed through the cypress trees
to the hill path followed by a dog.

Timed to half an hour.
From the next mountain range he watched
the city ride a gold sea, and sink,
then walked towards the next valley,
a civilization murmuring in his briefcase.

# ALASDAIR MACLEAN

## Sea and Sky

Sea and sky. Earthbound as I am
I've never yet been able to decide
which one I like best. I'd live,
I think, for preference on the sea.
I'd farm there a more fruitful soil
than what surrounds me here.
I'd be a connoisseur of gulls
and every day I'd open a new horizon.

I'd choose the sky for burial,
though, if such were possible.
I'd have mountains at my head and feet.
When Gabriel blew his trumpet I'd arrive
before God's kindness became strained.
The clouds would ease my bones
more than the hard rocks of Ardnamurchan.
Not worms would feed on me but larks.


## Rams

Their horns are pure baroque,
as thick at the root as a man's wrist.
They have golden eyes and roman noses.
All the ewes love them.

They are well equipped to love back.
In their prime they balance;
the sex at one end of their bodies
equalling the right to use it at the other.

When two of them come face to face
in the mating season
a spark jumps the gap.
Their heads drive forward like cannon balls.
Solid granite hills splinter into echoes.

They never wrestle, as stags and bulls do.
They slug it out. The hardest puncher wins.
Sometimes they back up so far for a blow
they lose sight of one another
and just start grazing.

They are infinitely and indefatigably stupid.
You can rescue the same one
from the same bramble bush
fifty times.
Such a massive casing to guard such a tiny brain—
as if Fort Knox were built to house a single penny!

But year by year those horns add growth.
The sex is outstripped in the end;
the balance tilts in the direction of the head.
I found a ram dead once.
It was trapped by the forefeet
in the dark water of a peatbog,
drowned before help could arrive
by the sheer weight of its skull.
Maiden ewes were grazing near it,
immune to its clangorous lust.
It knelt on the bank, hunched over its own image,
its great head buried in the great head facing it.
Its horns, going forward in the old way,
had battered through at last to the other side.

## Death of an Old Woman

She lived too much alone to be aware of it,
in a cottage on a stretch of moor,
built before the distant road was built
and shunned by everything built since.
Her croft had faded through the years
for lack of drainage and proper food,
bled of its green until the eye
could hardly tell where it began or ended.
Her house had a hole in the thatch
to let the smoke out—when there was any—
and the rain in, and three small openings
in the walls, two for light and one for charity,
and all about the size she was accustomed to.
The man who found her dead was drawn
in that direction by the movement.
That was the door of her empty henhouse
flapping in the wind, a nerve continuing to twitch.
She herself was lying in her bed,
causing a slight ripple in the blankets.
She had an English bible in her hands,
upside down. The doctor who examined her
stated that her mouth was full of raw potato.

## At the Peats

In March we start our harvesting.
We dig ourselves down out of sight
in a peatbog
and will carry on perhaps all year,

when the weather lets us,
till the job is done.
My father and myself.
We work in harmony,
he cutting and I spreading,
backwards and forwards,
up and down,
the rhythm of the cradle.
Then in May the sun comes north,
thawing out the silence,
and the tourists sprout.
They prod us with their cameras,
making us aware of what we do,
and once we appeared in *The Scottish Field*
in a photograph
so clear you could count the midges.
*Highland peasants cutting peat.*
*The abundance of free fuel*
*is an important factor in the crofting economy.*
One of my father's rare grim smiles,
like a lull in the east wind,
broke out when I read that to him.


## *The Beach in Winter*


Where every yard of ground was civilized
by deckchairs, there's nothing now
to cushion me from metaphor. A gull,
at my approach, hurls itself
into the wind and is knocked sideways
by the impact. In the shallows,

In the backwash of each wave,
long arms of tangle heave above the surface,
signal once or twice and disappear.
And higher up the beach I note
a certain kind of wading bird that runs
among the debris, scavenging the outgoing tide,
methodically turning over small stones.

## *Snaring Rabbits*

The snaring is an excuse, really.
It is the killing,
the moment when I fuse with God,
that makes the morning.
I hold the rabbit up by the hindlegs,
like an obstetrician holding up a baby.
One sharp chop to the nape,
my fingers stiffened
and pressed together for maximum impact.
The spine snaps.
The head flies back,
brushing against my knuckles,
before it falls again to dangle slackly
at the end of a hollow tube of skin.
The rabbit's pliable now.
The head will tuck in neatly
between the forelegs
and that's important
for my bag won't hold a full-length rabbit.
I pop it in and I'm finished.
One more, one less.

I coil the snare carefully,
trying not to kink the wire,
then on with my drooling hands
to the next burrow.


## *Horizons*

I was born
in sight of a horizon
and everywhere I go now
I hold my neighbourhood
up to the light.
If there's a black line
through the middle of it,
it's genuine.


## *Tallyman*

It must be easily
the hottest day so far this year.
Along the crest of the Glendryan Hills
the grass snaps under my feet.
If it were dark the rocks would glow.

I see the flies and hear them
before I see the sheep they quarrel over.
A cloud of bluebottles
thick enough to cast a shadow.
When she moves off at my approach
they rev up and follow.

Maggots, of course. You could scoop them
off her back in handfuls.
Small carnivorous worms with non-stop appetites,
they worry her to death.
The flies wait for the bones.

Sheep die unnoticed as a rule.
I was lucky to come across this one.
They go apart when their time comes
but without knowing why. They die instinctively.

I fan myself with my notebook.
It was cooler after all at sea level.
A stray bluebottle
follows me persistently all the way down.


## *Three-legged Frog*

A frog emerges from the fallen hay
that lies beneath my scythe,
trailing its right hindleg behind it,
joined now only by a strip of skin.

What must it be like
to be without a limb?

I balance experimentally on one foot.
The frog lurches towards a ditch,
its severed member banging
uselessly against its body,
a traveller with an empty suitcase.

## *Fishing*

We fish
in a sea worn smooth by last week's gales,
so flat and glassy
that if you breathed on it, it would mist.
There's no depth to it.
When I lean over the side
someone drops a weighted hook towards me.
Fish should come
through the hole he makes in my skull
but none do.
In the bottom of the boat
there lies just one small mackerel,
caught hours ago,
its colours dulled by its long immersion.

My father leans back on the oars;
a touch now and again is all he needs
to keep us stem-first to the tide.
His left hand knows what his right is doing.
'When I was young,' he says, 'it was worthwhile.'
He casts his mind back into the past
and fish after fish rises to the kill.
The deeper he goes the bigger they get.
When he was a boy
they were as tall almost as himself.
'It was before your time,' he says.
'It was before the trawlers came.'

Yes. I know about the trawlers.
I pretend to be examining my coat sleeve
but am really looking at my watch.

'There will be time,' it says, 'before your time,'
but when I breathe on it, it mists.
A catspaw dances across the water.
The Atlantic opens one eye, then goes back to sleep.


## Among Ourselves

Among ourselves we rarely speak.
Our tongues are thick with custom.
Inside our house, at this time of the year,
there's only the ticking of the clock
and the click of my mother's needles
as she knits herself away from where
she cast on. My father's pages rustle.
He makes himself a nest of newspaper.
I sit in a corner, smoking. Every time
I draw on my cigarette I hear
the tiny hiss of tobacco becoming ash.


## Death of a Hind

The hind, knocked sprawling by my shot,
rises, and weaves about the clearing
like a stage drunk going round a lamppost.
But when I arrive, panting, at her side
she marshals her straying legs and lines
them up beneath her in a last-ditch effort
at sobriety of direction. It's no use.

Some instinct points her at the fleeing herd
but only her will gallops. While I sweat,
curse, and tear at the jammed spent cartridge
she waits, patient now, wielding her dignity.
I clear the jam at last. My bullet,
sawn off at the tip, punches into her.
It unclenches its fist inside her heart.


## *The Old Dog*

Useless.
Our shouts bounce off him.
His eyes, each pasted over
with cataract,
tilt upwards
to the surreptitious claps
that span his days.
The furniture,
he finds,
is still predictable;
the people never were.
Inevitably
we get under his feet.
We curse him and keep him.

# WES MAGEE

## Maybe I'd do Well in Tibet

       Not for me
those half-baked noons in Sicily
weakly agog as a snake eases
its hot body from a fissured wall,
       or
all that bawling of verse at the wind
as it scoured the Lake District fells
and writing writing in a storm of creation,
       or even
ripping it up with mad Mike H
and the children of Albion
at pop-etry gigs in university halls!

       Such distances!
       Such energy!
       Such action!

       For me
the formalities of travel stifle,
and personal appearances
before Nature or students cost
much more than a bottle of Scotch!
       I'm plainly
for the poet keeping his cool in the city,
being steady in the isolation
of his mortgaged box,
a monk without privilege or position,
solitary in his cell,
above the yelping and the traffic snarl.

## 'Sunday Morning'

Sunday morning
>     and the sun
>     bawls
>     with
>     his big mouth

Yachts

>     paper triangles
>     of white and blue
>     crowd the sloping bay
>     appearing motionless
>     as if stuck there
>     by some infant thumb
>
>     beneath a shouting sky
>
>     upon a painted sea


## The Holiday, and After

He left suit and stiff collar behind,
   put on red jeans, hat, tattered vest,
and dug praties in wildest Ireland.

  Blue winds sliced through the hills,
the peat bog sucked and settled lower
  in its ancient bed

and in two weeks he grew a new face,
   took on the skin of a creature
making out in the wilderness.

   Back at the Bank he flicked notes
with a pimpled rubber thumb
   and ticked off the days

on a company calendar
   as the ice battalions of Winter
advanced across the town.

   And then, while stacking others' cash,
he felt the walls of commerce split
   and through the cracks

watched the new beasts come.
   In the cage of his chest
his heart thumped like a bunched fist

   as he saw them come on slow
through rough streets littered with whitening bones
   and the first of a new year's snow.


## *The Radish*

   I'm a left wing radish, raw and
red as a thumped nose, body scabbed
where dirt hurt. It was you who set

   me down in that regimented
plot where I knew the poverty
of stones, grew up under the superb

stars, and felt waters freeze in my
head. But I survived that waste land
for you to rip me out when I

sprouted messages of a green
spring to come. You raped my family,
tore up the roots, transported us

to this fearful kitchen camp and
dropped me, castrated and scoured, bald
as a cold sun, on to this white plate.

I see you coming, mouth alive
with tortures, itching to screw my
groin in salt, but when I open

my heart and broken lie in the
folded flag of your tongue then will
my whiteness bite, bite finally.


## *Today's Lesson: an Observation*

A group of teachers, on a refresher course, visit a model school.

Today let's catch some common crawlies. First
we'll place traps in likely places—long grass,
bushes, by bricks—burying jars in the
earth till only their lips show. By morning
we'll have a large collection to observe.
Time then to construct wormeries and glass
vivariums.

The field was threadbare from
football and dried by a long summer. Ants
welled up from the earth, crazily into
bright day. Pop-eyed we bombed them amongst their
red brethren and waited for war. Then an
ambush for a dazzled earwig—its body
gobbled by the dusty backed ants! And green,
juicy caterpillars—dozens!—herded
into a chalk corral and those that crossed
the line—pulped! The perimeter gradually
swamped in yellow pus!

                      Wormeries are
possible in bell jars. Earth layers, thus,
stony soil, up through clay to garden dirt.
The worms will slowly ravel this and don't
let the children maltreat life, however mean.
We can show its beauty through a glass pane.
Take, for instance, this woodlouse and note its
graceful ways.

                    It seemed we grew from violence
to violence. A rat on a tip caught broadside
with a brick. Arrows, steel-headed, thwacked heart-deep
into a pond toad. All those sun dried deaths
and moony actions. Our secret tortures
and dreams of graveyard murders—yet we left
humans well alone!

                    Well now, coffee, but
first a chance to see some group activity.
Ah, Miss Thing, all right? Observe the work!
The care that I can only name as love!

Oh yes, they work. Pinafored in white, like
surgeons, they handle mice attentively,
learning that what's good for smaller fry is
fine for us, and how to make the educated
guess when things go wrong. And their desire to
scatter limbs like straw? They smile and answer
breathily—in fact more free than my lot.
But coffee calls. Now will some cherub test
a beetle's back and stare intently as the
shard cracks in her hand? Miss Thing, I think, would
know. Some tautness in her smile tells tales of
blood before we ambled on this scene. Her
eyes recount an ancient gothic story,
printed in blood, staked out deep in the heart.

## *Happening*

One, with a Mohican scalp, blew
mad things on a sax. Another,
acne red, piledrove a piano

while the audience jumped in with
drums, newspaper rolls, transistors,
cans. Tomatoes bombed and splashed their

blood against walls, foreheads. Then the
hard stuff; spinning spuds and, strangely,
a cabbage which turned and turned like

a green angel. The hall shook in
a barrage of noise and mixed veg.
Twenty minutes of this and we

ambled off to a pub and jugged
up to the full. In all a rowdy
success. It seems a caretaker,

moaning, came and cleaned up the mess.


## *Postcard from a Long Way Off*

    We have arrived,
fallen out from forests, by an unknown route.
The past has been a nightmare of blizzards and
lice in the folds of the flesh. We have come through
virgin lands, hidden deep in drifts, and finally
crept past the ice locked outposts of a bad age.

    For the moment
we are secure, holed up in this ancient house.
The walls are waterfalls, the rats ignore us
having long forgotten humans and how to fear.
Huddled we sit, staring to recall that crawl
past warning sheets like crows hung dead from trees.

    The window is
a joke. I can blot it out with my hand. And
was that a bird falling? Did its wing rip and
the gale turn on it, howling like a Chinese
legend knifing through the blood? And why, out here,
do wind and world thrash out a frantic ice age war?

    Tomorrow? We
journey on. We are supplied with hunger and
memories which still rub sore. Yet something makes

us move, some force which clamps down tight the black ice
wilderness takes whips and drives us on towards
the spaces where only the white noise hurtles.


## *Junior Junkies*

During the summer
the kids collected
pickle jars, cornflake
boxes, cogs, hauling
them dead from dustbins,

and now the school's back
they treat it like a
tip, heaping junk in
a corner of the
class. On this we're hooked:

kids everywhere with
mad machines, strange fish,
and soon the room's a
thunderstuck dump. From
trash creations grow.

Then in the spring a
vast display complete
with coloured cards (*Jill
Miles*, ' *A Plug Hole Man*')
and soon a ritual

ripping and, yes, a
bonfire on the field.
*What's next? What now?* they
shout, and there we go,
another junkie

quest. And if, next term
you ask them what they'd
liked, it's *Oh yes, it
all was good, but we
loved the burning best!*


## *Knowing*


    Somewhere
in his after silence
I perceive the point
lying in ripeness
   beyond sown words.

    Smoking
we watch elastic ghosts
swim for the ceiling
and I roll the germ
   of truth till it

holds like
dough in the mouth. The dried
leaves take calm hold and
I see my listening
   has spirited

      me into
the flower of knowing,
down past the earth's crust,
back through time, into
    the seed itself.


## *The Name Game*

We talked casually about
P. G. Wodehouse saying that
Jeeves, like Winter, had come round
again, and then played a ploy
where everyone had to list
Beckett's plays in a droll way,
punning his spudgy titles.

On the tennis lawn a bird
stopped: the gale fluting its tail.
*'Black-backed gull!'* someone said
as another grabbed a book and
informed us of the facts of
its life. The bird bent off into
the wind, and even that's

like Ted Hughes, it was remarked.
We watched, achingly secure
in our fixed smiles, the easy chairs,
waiting for snow, or Proust to
be remembered by some wag,
knowing that knowing the name
is the main part of the game.

# PETE MORGAN

# *Disguise*

Having penetrated my disguise
with lengths of predictable steel
and not a little wit
they
in their indefinite wisdom
scoured my skin with intricate designs
of their own choosing.
Having failed to obliterate
their scars with numberless
additional disguises
and frequent unsuccessful experiments
with Water Fire & Love
I discovered
somewhat later
and quite by accident
that each scar was moveable.
Ahah! Carefully now
and in complete privacy
I moved the markings
over my body and slid them
one by one
into the darkness inside my head
and very much out of sight.

Children
you need no longer be afraid
you can have a laugh with Lumpy now
come closer—
look at my disguise
never let me catch you
looking in my eyes.

# The White Stallion

There was that horse
  that I found then
  my white one
big tall and lean as
  and mean as hell.

And people who saw me
  would stare as I passed them
  and say
    'Look at him . . .
    how he rides his cock-horse.'
But my steed
  the white stallion
stormed into the moonlight
  and on it was me.

There were those girls
  that I found then
  my loved ones
small fat and mean ones
  and virgins as well.

And those girls who saw me
  would weep as I passed them
  and cry
    'Look at him . . .
    how he rides his cock-horse.'
But my steed
  the white stallion
went proud in the still night
  and on it was me.

There was one girl
  that I loved then—
  a woman—
as tall and as lithe as
  a woman should be.

And soon as I saw her
  I dismounted my stallion
  to stay
    by the woman
  whose love I required
But my steed
  the white stallion
rode off in the moonlight
  and on it was she.

Goodbye to the horse
  to the woman
  and stallion.
Farewell to my cock-horse
  and loving as well.

To people who see me
  and stare as I pass them
  I wail
    'Look at me . . .
    I once rode a cock-horse.'
But my steed
  the white stallion
is lost in the moonlight
  and on it rides she.

## The Red Monkey Poems

I

Again the red monkey is in turmoil
beginning to move again
move slowly monkey
*Ahah!* monkey
Good monkey
monkey
monkey

*rien ne va plus*, monkey

II

Again the red monkey moves
his hot mouth pressed
against the dome his
pink paws scratch
for a firm
hold

take it easy monkey
take care now monkey
take your time monkey
easy monkey
easy

monkey, don't fall.

### III

Inside his hidy-hole
        the red monkey moves
        (like a silent movie)
monkey
monkey
don't dance, monkey

*the red monkey is a fair dancer*

### IV

Give the red monkey lights
Give the red monkey lights
Give the red monkey lights

he breaks, starry.

### V

The small lips suckle at the warm wall
which has no corners

move round the wall/monkey
move round the wall

it is
dark

somewhere.

# The Rainbow Knight's Confession

My armour *becomes* me.
I have it to the letter now—
even the colour of my steed,
a much deliberated
white.

    When black becomes the colour of the good
    I shall ride black.
    In the meantime
    piebalds are for taking.

My helmet is of *catholic* proportions—
nothing fancy—just the stoutest tin
and not too loud for roustabouts to clang.

My visor's of an intricate design—
so I see out and no one else sees in.

    I carry colours more than arms
    but that is for the better
    if there's challenge in the air.
    My colours won't offend—
    with rainbows there.

    I change my colour for my company—
    a purple knight sees purple in my cloth
    a yellow knight sees yellow
    blue knight blue
    the blackest knights I raise my visor to.

I wear my stirrups midway
from my girth—wanting not
to offend the gentlemen of court
who tell the talents of a man
from being short on strappage
else too long, and therefore foolish—
and all of that through armour.

There is no doubt I cut a pretty rig
I am saluted more than I salute—
which is as it should be.

My breast-plate is most carefully prepared
with daily rubs of talcum and such tricks.
I make not too much noise—
with oils from Persia I have learnt
to cut out all my jangle, squeak and clank.
I hear more times than I am heard.

I have my hauberk metalled to a T
and all in all the time is going well.
Only in my private chambers
do I stand apart from this.
I place my armour in the corner then
or else I'm working on its gleam.

O sure, this armour's only implement.
I mind my body too—
rub oils in that
and pare it where it grows.
I bathe it daily,
daily shave my chin.

There's nothing else except the hair of it
and I have learnt a trick or two with that—
*I comb it, where it grows, across my horns.*

## *One of them was washing 'His' body in Milk*

One of them was washing '*His*' body in Milk
he trembled
he was endlessly whistling
& continually repeating to himself
*Milk . . . Milk . . .*
*Good Milk*
& he wanted very much to become clean.

He had two hands
and a quantity of Milk
which he carefully rubbed
into '*His*' body.
He paid particular attention to
'*His*' body
& he wanted very much to become clean.

He stood trembling
in the centre of the room
and carefully dried '*His*' white body
repeating to himself
*Milk . . . Milk . . .*
*Good Milk*
& he wanted very much to become clean.

## *Pierre the Fibster Lives*

Pierre the Fibster habitates a tree
says it's a good life up there
calls his body
We.

We . . .
shall have a good time
says Pierre
We . . .
enjoy the open air.

Pierre
Pierre
come down please
only crows & cattle
habitate the trees.


## *Wall*

I built a cell of coolest stone.
I did not build it exactly—
I made it what it was.

I stood inside it
a sun-coloured prisoner
in shackles of the purest gold
in milk-white chains
of ivory.

I fashioned for it
certain comforts—
hasps of saffron, walls of watchet,
a yoke of lapis lazuli.

I made the ceiling darkest blue:
Only the brighter stars shone through.

I built a cell of coolest stone:
Inside I stood like wood against the window
a band of white across my eyes.

*God bless Peter, God bless Paul,*
*God bless everyone except the wall.*

## & the Grey Mare being the better Steed

It was quick & easy
an easy choice to take
best to ride the better steed
& the grey mare being the better steed
an easy choice to make.

It was nice & easy
an easy chance to break
best to take the softer fall
& the short fall being the softer fall
an easy fall to fake.

It was free & easy
an easy life to take
best to kill the fatter calf
& the fat calf being the fatter calf
an easy feast to make.

# PAUL MULDOON

## *The Inheritors*

Where the mushrooms are blundering and blunting out of
 the Curragh dung
They are the little glazed earthenware bowls out of the kiln

And the tiny lamps of the early Christians littering these
 dark graves
Are of the soft red rock yet they are fragile as eggshells

Where the flames of the yolks have been blown out by a
 boy and the tiny lamps
And the skulls and the bulbs on the ceiling of the same red
 rock

As the floor remind me of how we must go underground
 out of the daylight
To watch the growth of the mushrooms they are not the
 wind

The leader of our group speaks English he has brought us
 back to where we started
To the soft mouth and no matter how often we have spent
 the day

Against the mushrooms and have slammed the door on the
 desolation of severed necks
They will have pushed up as many or more by the follow-
 ing morning

Though they had been buried by the skittering lethal flints

## Stillborn

You were first.
The ewe lapped ochre and lake
But you would not move.
Weighted with stones yet
Dead your dead head floats.

Better dead than sheep,
The thin worm slurred in your gut,
The rot in your feet,
The red dog creeping at dawn.
Better than dipped in the hard white water,
Your stomach furred,
Your head hardboiled.

Better dead than dyed
In a bowl of pale whin petals.
Better than rolling down the hill,
Pale skull flaking.
First to break.
First for the scream of the clean bite.
Better dead with your delph head floating.

## Unborn

(for Seamus Heaney)

It has become a part
Of me. I might try to abort

The poem. No one would know
But myself. God I should have known

Never again to start
A poem. Now that the start

Is made, I have no right
To say the end. No right.

I am pregnant a day
And must not call it a day.

I know its birth
But not its date of birth.

Then the poem will live, will live
Outside my life.

I will wrap
It in paper. Leave it on your step.


## *Skeffington's Daughter*

An Iron Maiden, brainchild of the Lieutenant of the Tower under Henry the Eighth.

Not one to lose her head,
Her father had thought. Now her lover
Had left her pregnant, he still thought he understood

Her want. Being his daughter, she must have
Another chance. No one would suffer.
It would be nothing like a death

In the family. Leaving the backstreet and foetus
Behind her, she would still be taken for a clever,
Careful virgin. Not one to lose face.

## *Snail*

I guessed the letter must be yours.
I recognized the cuttle ink,
The serif on the P.
I read the postmark and the date.
I would not open it just yet,
Impatience clamped beneath a paperweight.
I took your letter at eleven
To the garden with my tea.
And suddenly the yellow gum
Secreted halfway up a damson bush
Had grown a shell.
I let the folded pages fall
And took a stick to break its hold.
I turned it over through the grass
To watch your mouth withdraw.

## *Hedgehog*

The snail moves
Like a hovercraft,
Held up by a rubber
Cushion of itself, sharing its secret

With the hedgehog. The hedgehog
Shares its secret with no one.
We say, 'Hedgehog, come out
Of yourself and we will love you.

We mean no harm. We want
Only to listen to what
You have to say. We want
Your answers to our questions.'

The hedgehog gives nothing
Away, keeping itself to itself.
We wonder what a hedgehog
Has to hide, why it so distrusts.

We forget the God
Under this crown of thorns.
We forget that never again
Will a God trust in the world.


## *The Indians On Alcatraz*

Through time their sharp features have softened and blurred
As if they still inhabited the middle distance,

As if these people have never stopped riding hard
In an opposite direction, the people of the broken lances

Who have seemed forever going back. Now they have
    willed this reservation,
It is as if they accept that they are islanders at heart,

As if this island running away to sea and seed, bartered
For with bright trinkets, has forever been the faroff
    destination

Of the bands of little figures on horseback returning,
    returning.
After the newspaper and television reports I remark

On how people can still be themselves, but each morning
Leaves me more grateful for the fact that they never attack
    after dark.

## Poem for Lawrence

'If men were as much men as lizards are lizards they'd be worth looking at.'     *Lizard*, D. H. LAWRENCE

In the dampness,
It seems as if termites,
White ants, keen in this pylon.

Yesterday a man was harnessed
Up there, spinning wire. Spider.
Yet mantoothed maneyed

Caucasian male. He could not help
Doing his own thing.
Chameleons do not think themselves worth looking at,

Preferring to be thought of,
Not as lizards, but rocks, leaves, jerboa droppings.
In the dampness they put out their tongues

At termites, white ants. Men.

## Wind and Tree

In the way that most of the wind happens where there are
     trees
Most of the world is centred about ourselves.

Sometimes when the wind has thrown them together and
     together
One tree will take another in her arms and hold.

But their branches that now are rubbing madly together
     and together
Are making no real fire, they are bruising each other.

Sometimes I think I ought to be like a single tree, going
     nowhere,
Since my own arm cannot and will not break the other.

Yet by my broken bones I know new weather.


## The Charcoal Burner

He thought, I am like a fire,
There may be people near yet they are far.

He thought, I am an element,
The want to be myself, myself, is my only want,

I need only keep the fire alight.

So he stifled the fire with soil,
From its burning slowly, slowly, there was charcoal,

He wrote with charcoal on a stone.
But by now the fire could not live by fire alone,

The fire was out, the fire was out.


## *Marble Orchard*

(Marble Orchard is American slang for a cemetery.)

I used to think that there was something somehow makeshift
About this hive that has been all your own work
But now that I have removed the flimsy lid I know your gift
Of sugarcake to be only the tip of the iceberg

For the sugar was willed by the bees it was not a gift
And though you built the hive it is no longer all your own work

And love we need fear no wintering sniggering bees that steer
Faster and more deadly than the driven snow but fear
Because we are human and again perhaps because we are lovers
Only the orchard not the same as this which may later fill with pears

And which the bees might consider a change for better or
    worse
While we because our love is human continue to succumb

To the thought of our final years and final days and final
    hours
When we might reconsider our description of the womb
As an inverted pear and as the bees may well have done in
    our final hours
We might conclude that a pear is the inverted womb

## *Aubade*

A bat from the back
   Of your throat, the cry could take
To the air and flick

Passionless and blind
   From wall to wall, the thin sound
Of the blonde doll turned

Over on her back,
   Your smalled cry automatic,
Your hair synthetic

I thought hay to wind
   In a soft tether, but found
That as the hay turned

Into rope, I backed,
   Back and back, far as your look,
The length of my lack.

## Hedges in Winter

Every year they have driven stake after stake after stake
Deeper into the cold heart of the hill.
Their arrowheads are more deadly than snowflakes,
Their spearheads sharper than icicles,

Yet stilled by snowflake, icicle.
They are already broken by their need of wintering,
These archers taller than any snowfall
Having to admit their broken shafts and broken strings,

Whittling the dead branches to the girls they like.
That they have hearts is visible,
The nests of birds, these obvious concentrations of black.
Yet where the soldiers will later put on mail,

The archers their soft green, nothing will tell
Of the heart of the mailed soldier seeing the spear he flung,
Of the green archer seeing his shaft kill.
Only his deliberate hand, a bird pretending a broken wing.


## The Electric Orchard

The early electric people domesticated the wild ass;
They had experience of falling off.
Occasionally, they might have fallen out of the trees;
Climbing again, they had something to prove

To their neighbours. And they did have neighbours;
The electric people lived in villages
Out of their need of security and their constant hunger.
Together they learned to divert their energies

To neutral places; anger to the banging door,
Passion to the kiss.
And electricity to earth. Having stolen his thunder
From an angry God, through the trees

They had learned to string his lightning.
Burying the electric-poles
Waist-deep in the clay, they stamped the clay to healing;
Diverting their anger to the neutral,

The electric people were confident, hardly proud.
They kept fire in a bucket,
Boiled water and dry leaves in a kettle, watched the lid
By the blue steam lifted and lifted.

So that, where one of the electric people happened to fall,
It was accepted as an occupational hazard;
There was something necessary about the thing. The North
    Wall
Of the Eiger was notorious for blizzards;

If one fell there, his neighbour might remark, 'Bloody fool'.
All that would have been inappropriate,
Applied to the experienced climber of electric-poles.
'I have achieved this great height';

No electric person could have been that proud.
Forty feet, often not that,
If the fall happened to be broken by the roof of a shed.
The belt would break, the call be made,

The ambulance arrive and carry the faller away
To hospital with a scream.
There and then the electric people might invent the railway,
Just watching the lid lifted by the steam;

Or decide that all laws should be based on that of gravity,
Just thinking of the faller fallen.
Even then, they were running out of things to do and see;
Gradually, they introduced legislation

To cover every conceivable aspect of the electric-pole.
They would prosecute any trespassers;
The high-up singing and alive fruit liable to shock or kill
Were forbidden. Deciding that their neighbours

And their neighbours' innocent children ought to be stopped
For their own good, they planted fences
Of barbed-wire around the electric-poles. None could
    describe
Electrocution, falling, innocence.

# WILLIAM PESKETT

## *simile: you are*

you are as infinite as the skyparabola
oh how
you drive me to simile out of
my head as smokey as a foxglove wing
out of my head you glide
as pacific as a treacle steamer
coasting on the empire line


## *The question of time*

Where on earth
has the stumbling mammoth gone?
that giant tripper over nations
who used to think
the world was his
after the succulent brontosaurus.

The ages shed no tears for me.
I am not their resting
but their passing through,
left to watch
the intricate bees
in their noble art of dance.

## Guns

Everybody knows that guns were invented
by the Chinese,
guaranteed not to explode unexpectedly
previous to depressing
that little lever below the barrel,
now called the trigger.

Everybody knows how you put in those bullet-
shaped objects
and that you point the open end
at the person you hate
and then how you squint down the barrel
and softly pull the trigger.

Everybody knows from the cowboy films
that there is a kick
and the bullet spurts away with an angelic bang.
They know so well
how the man grunts and falls badly
to the ground.

But how many people, do you think,
know that if you stick
the open end of the gun (invented by the Chinese)
into your mouth
and coyly pull the trigger
you hardly hear the bang at all?

You just see
the rich foaming blood,
spat on the floor, for a split-second.

## *Impressionist Landscape*

the mountains are mauve
and fishermen are scattered
paintbox remnants
from a primeval afternoon

birds hang in the sky
in an emulsion—
they knew more freedom
in the tethered wombegg
of their primordial nest

the sun is a canary smudge
on the brink of a molten lake
and the leaves on the trees
know nothing—
not even how to be leaves


## *Plants*

Plants have the sexless advantage
of being silent.
They ignore the bees
which blunder like tactless cupids
from man to wife,
remaining haughty witnesses
to their own annual
pollination rigmarole.

There is no vegetable whisper
of endearment in the beds:
the plants part their petals
indifferently, quite aware
of their identical beauty.
Plants are mutely earnest, practical;
they communicate their love
by circumstance.


## *rainbow*


rainbow youre a twofaced sort
of fellow
youre a warped candybar
and the sun uses you
as a weapon against the shadow
of the rain

rainbow youre not a selfmade
chap atall
youre just a compound of enemies
and the only reason
anybody likes you is because without you
theyd be nothing

## *exodus*

the dove has left the hand
like a thrown dead bird
sucked into the sky.
the hand drops down
and the head is bowed;
the sunken eyes
are lowered to the sun.

the dying corpses on the tower
are picked and torn.
bodies do not bleed:
their hands are veined like leaves.
the vulture's heads
nod and tear the spirit
from down the brown meat hollow.

the sun has dried the bone
and vultures leave on skeletal wings.
no muscle strains to bid farewell:
the hands have dropped and
only the clean bowed head
with sunken eyes like leaves
watches from the grating's tissue.

## *crayfish facts 1–4*

i cant help but admire the crayfish
with its hide like crackling.

its antennae are red like scalded
cocktail grasses.

you couldnt pierce the crayfish
with a bowie spike.

it lives in a beautiful fluid garden.
its eyes are very small.

## *soldier*

deep in the trench stink
rifle smoke rises like fuse wire,
insulating the army lines.

in the mud a sadeyed soldier dies,
his crumpled leg bones
stemming from his boots.

## *I'll watch my friend, the moving mountain*

I'll watch my friend, the moving mountain
Until the earth's burnt core
Has ceased to shine.

I'll watch my friend, the moving mountain
Which told me
It would never try
To fool itself by growing
Taller than the reach of hand or eye.

I'll watch my friend, the moving mountain
Until the grass which lawns
Its face has died,
And till I see
My craggy friend has lied.

## *Dead man in a sunset*

Apple-heavy, the sun
which feeds the skies
along its eastern stem
is falling, and in falling cries.

I, alone, can live
the dusk whose night
can't let the living see
its falling or its dying light.

## *sandscape*

somewhere between the sea
and the tide's last lick
a woman lies,
too awkward to be sleeping.

approach her like a bishop,
there is no need to hurry:
there is no blood—
the sea will never use
a murder weapon except
his own embrace.
look, her face is white
as beeswax.

her belly seems pregnant
and helpless
as if her duty were the sea's
vast procreation.

do not touch her flesh,
it looks quite real
but splits like custard skin.
it is the reality
which makes you smooth her hair.

it is wrong to pity her,
look at her eyes.

do not think of her as carrion
but stare into the sea
as she did,
drowning, living
all her life.

## *Moths*

Moths are hopeless in the air,
they are wild uncomfortable
companions to the wind,
enjoying the randomness of flight.

Moths have no face.
Smiling, I always think
they must drink light.
A cloud of them can absorb the moon.

The female moth is like the male.
When you crush it,
it doesn't bleed—
it sprinkles your hands with talcum.


## *Why I am the Last of the World's Great Lovers*

when shadowboxing in the saturday backstalls
an extrafeature sometimes flicks
across my mind
its a shame nobody seems to be wearing
clown lipstick anymore
or rolling soft makeeyes in silent scenes
and nobody ever holds a girl
the way they used to

nobody does a silken swoon
across the railroad track anymore
or commits one of those flash
honkytonk suicides

everybodys forgotten that valentino was once
the coming soon at their local odeon
and that his coffin was buried
in pink reincarnations and cards saying
                come back valentino
see you in heaven
one day ill request his second showing
with dubbed stereophonic keyboards
and fill the kinema with my children
announcing
by way of explanation that this
perhaps is why i
am the last of the worlds great lovers


*Crom—April 1969*

    the lake plane slices
    the land from its reflection
    like a fin.

    on a still day
    there is twice as much of everything
    except ripples.

# RICHARD RYAN

## *Knockmany*

(For John Montague)

In slow procession
trees ascend
the hill, enter
the mist-held ring
to crowd, chanting,
around the silent
hive of stones.

Giant tree-priests,
slowly they rock
in prayer; searching
the earth, long root
veins writhe down-
ward, probing
for blood the deep

hill's heart. As
the quick sap stirs,
runnels upward
through trunk and
thigh, filling
with its white life
the glistening loins,

louder the branches,
bone-hard arms
dipping, digging
up air, moan—
mad with certainty—
as the mist,
prised up like a stone,

reveals a monstrous
shadow rising, rising
through the forked, skin-
less fingers—the
swaying trees lean
forward, clutching that
shape, *humming, humming* . . .

## *The Thrush's Nest*
(For Michael Kinsella)

Bramble, like barbed wire,
Stitches the thicket tight, laces
A net of leaves against the
Sun: only the birds can pass.

Pinned high where the twigs
Cross, it shapes from a blur;
Still heart of the bush, darkness
Parts slowly to let it through.

Her black pebble-eyes dazed
With waiting, the mother snaps
Alive at my presence, grabs
Air, screaming—reveals her shining

Hoard: luminous with heat,
Four freckled ovals of perfect
Sky, the skin of one threaded
With cracks—pulsing with life.

## A Heap of Stones

I asked directions
at a farmhouse door:
they pointed to a field
high on the hillside
where they said
the Giant's Grave
stood, and waited,
watching by their gate,
an old man
and his wife, watching
till I turned the road,
wondering perhaps why
a man would climb
half a mountain to see
a heap of stones.

Over the ditch and through
the rising bog spotted
with tiny spits of wild cotton
I moved, a mile
an hour, until the land
below became a mood,
long shadows sweeping
inland, eating light . . .

Armed with bright pictures
of club and claw
I searched until suddenly
it grinned at me:
filling the hole in a crazy hedge
it overflowed into the field—

great tables impaled
upon a pencil of stone;
a tabernacle of ancient death
dug deep as an evil eye
in the skull of the hill.
I banished urgent images
from my downward path and one
by one unclenched
the stone cold fingers round my brain.

## Viking Deposits

*1. Museum*
Bog fruit;
skinless, a
scrap of hair
and rotted
sword, contour
of skull; the
glass casket,
electric light:
the shape
roughly human.

*2. Trelleborg*
Silence. Cloud
hand shadows
grapple bald walls
and climb the
wind, walk over
Trelleborg;

deft sheep topple
dew-drops down
mounds; the silence,
so, is not soundless . . .

*3. Runestone*
Chant round
red fire,
flicker of lips
and toad
under wet stone:
blob eye
and ticking
heart slowly
staring the sun
down . . .

*4. The brain*
To mere, iron
on bone, to
mood mind
pulls the eye:
lithe-thighed
they step at dawn—
ravens wind high
and wait—in
the first crash
men fall . . .

bog fruit;
skinless, a
scrap . . .

## *Function*

Here
again,
those signals

from
below,
all else replaced

the
fierce pulse
rising to beat mind

down.
And I obey,
flesh seeking flesh

reduced
to function by
demand from below

the
floor of
life, that swirling

liquid
world where
the unborn swarm.

## *Moher*

The earth is
round all
right, but here

earth ends, thick
tongues of mist
licking the ledge.

A hiss—the sea
breathing? That
crying is not birds . . .

Thrown up screaming,
a chough, its claws
and beak blazing—

it grabs at light,
then topples shrieking
down out of the world.


## *From My Lai the Thunder went west*

and it all died down
to an underground
tapping and then that,
too, stopped dead.

In cornfield, wheat
field, a black
sheet of earth
was spread neatly

across the seed
they planted.
And the fields turn
daily to the sun.

Come high Summer
and the first shoots
will appear, puzzling
the sun as, growing

through earth, growing
through grass, the
human crop they have sown—
child bone, wife

bone, man
bone will stand
wavering in the pale fields:
the silent, eye-

less army will
march west through
Autumn and Europe
until, streaked

with December rain
they will stand in
New York and Texas;
as the lights click

out across America
they will fence in
that white house
tapping on window,

tapping on door. Till
dawn, then rain only:
from sea to sea drifting,
drops of bright ruby.


## *Galaxy*

faint
   in deep space,
      immense as a brain.

Down
   through the thought-
      shaft it drifts, a wale

of light to
   which the retina
      opens and is entered

time
   and space dis-
      appearing as the mind

recedes
   to a soundless
      flickering somewhere

deeper
   than consciousness
      where, permanent as

change
   a whorl of light
      rides, wheeling in darkness.

## *Ireland*

That ragged
leaking raft held
between sea and sea

its long
forgotten cable melting
into deeper darkness where,

at the root
of it, the slow
sea circles and chews.

Nightly the dark-
ness lands like hands
to mine downwards, springing

tiny leaks
till dawn finds
field is bog, bog lake.

# CLIVE WILMER

## Elegy for Donald Campbell

The courage to confront a world beyond
The bounded motion of the gradual day
Established an irrevocable bond
Between his will and powers that would repay

His tireless aspiration with a death.
He chose; and sought, upon the frontier
Between the light above and dark beneath,
Speed, in which he could act as sufferer

Yet drive the force behind the speed's increase.
Complete exposure to experience,
When time and normal laws of motion cease,
Brings the cold wind, the unmoving world, and chance

Headlong toward you in a storm of pain;
And exaltation. He heard the will's command
To fly and dive and smash the surface-pane,
To penetrate the dark, to never land.


## The Exile

I threw up watchtowers taller than my need
With bare walls the enemy could not scale,
I wrenched stone from the near country-side
And built my city on the highest hill;
    Over the land I scarred I reared
Impenetrable the walls and citadel.

Then to approach the city from afar
All you could see was soaring, there was such peace
Knowing the city mine I lay secure.
My own, one night, woke me—every face
    A jutting rock relief in glare,
The torchlight that illumined new distress.

They lit me into darkness. The harsh sun
—My understanding, dazzled when it dawned—
Disclosed me vulnerable. I stumbled on,
Till blown, a sterile seed, by years like wind
    Indifferent guidance, I am set down
Among familiar stone in a changed land.

Now it is only details I perceive:
The towers lopped, stone interspersed with weed
In patches; a deeper speckling seems to give
Form to the complex of decay, but is fled
    With a lizard flicker. Poppies revive,
In the wall they spatter, spectres of old blood.


## The Goldsmith

To stay anxiety I engrave this gold,
Shaping an amulet whose edges hold
A little space of order: where I find,
Suffused with light, a dwelling for the mind.

## Arthur Dead

Terror stalks this land where once King Arthur
    Ruled with virtue steeped in vision;
Now in restless vigil his knights quest, their impulse
    Dark obsession.

Yet those few, who halting at the wayside
    Kneel to victims of the terror,
Salvage thus, from desolation which they ride in,
    Love and honour.


## Octogenarian

The dead survive in words,
The dark beneath their light;
    Memory's shards
Are bright stars that compose the night.

The enchanted words she mutters
Summon from her deep past
    People and matter
Whose substance memories outlast.

Beyond fact, contemplating
Pageants that throng her thought—
    Her words creating
Pale shades of loves whose warmth they sought—

She lives entranced, but with
A cold weight on her mind
   That is not death,
That is the dead she cannot find.


## *The Stone Circle*

Upon a hill I stand alone
As centre to a ring of stone,
A point it seems where time's advance
Has been repelled, in part by chance,
In part by primitive design.

I strive to make their silence mine.

The energy of wind combined
With raging weathers of the mind
May well have been the powers that urged
Their placing here. Yet here submerged
Are all my energies and theirs
Who set these forms against the years,
Against their pain, against the wind;

Who long ago attained their end.

But living peace cannot endure although
   Endurance may be all we know
Of peace. While on the stones I meditate
   Leaves and the grass anticipate
Returning: the approaching gale of winter
   Makes me aware that I must enter

That colder world with which the birds contend
   Who lifted by the wind must bend
Their feathered weight against the elements.

I turn to face indifference.
But knowledge of a liberty I find
   Set down like stones within the mind;
That energy implicit in repose
   Is his, resilient, who knows
—As those who laid this silence must have known—
   Resistance to the wind, through stone.


## *Victorian Gothic*

(For Dick Davis)

Blackened walls: a Gothic height
Crouches and does not soar, locked
To the earth like slabs of outcrop stone
That touch no God; they imitate

Monoliths of the moors. Smokebound
Maze of streets in a northern town,
Low-skied misted marshland: ghosts
Haunt him, a grave imagination.

Mist merged with industrial smoke
Where the ghosts swim:
Their scrawny bodies topped with blackened heads
Like those that peer through jungle leaves.

Manufacturers, poets, moralists, colonizers, all
Engendered empires of despair
Built on blackness in the grey air.

What does the grey stone mask? Such battlements
Attest obscure defence.
                         His mind draws
Close to its melancholy: as
In dank winter to the heaped log-fire
Of a Saxon hall, beyond whose walls
What lurks in greyness?

Castles from dark days his reason
Girdles like siege but preserves,
Long years of siege that constitute defence;
Renascence ghosts, dark blood
Steams on the axe—industrial fumes
Dry the blood of the starved worker—marshland
Dank at sunset the sky bleeds
Pillarbox red.

## *The Well*

All day to gaze down into a well
as into yourself—as through self
to the blue sky fringed with green

of the world; and at length,
through a tunnelled forest of fronds that grow
from the mossy walls, to perceive

only your own face against the sky,
eyes glazed in contemplation, staring back
through a forest: is at large

to behold and desire to behold
—through foliage and from beyond darkness—
always, as in a well, meeting your stare,

your own face afloat on the surface,
with your thoughts bubbling from the deep spring
and your voice, reverberant, echoing response;

and to forget how without it
there is only the old perspective into endless dark
with silence at the source.


## *Ghost King*

My Father is a ghost King:
                      he resides
In the shade of green, rain-drenched trees
That steal warmth from the sun's heat.
His realm is silence, ancient repose:
In darkness beneath the shadows which these stones
—Time-moulded and moss-softened—
Lean over, he holds sway.

The stream that runs on past his grave
Is Time, that lulls him in his sleep
Breeding abundance.

England by day is a green silence;
And beneath the grass, it is history runs on by: until
Night and my Father
Consume it.

Rags of the dawn-mist
Or shreds of bonfire-smoke
Shroud his dwelling, he is a ghost King,
His daylight apparition is the rainbow.

But mostly, his soul rests
Under this hill crowned by the ancient church,
Where the dumb sheep attend him,
And sunlight flows like warm soft water over
Ancient sleep.

2.
Come the night storm he is less liberal.
There is a spirit on the wind: is the voice his
That is howling beyond his grave,
Over the ravaged waste his Lebensraum—
Or the night air itself
In the bare branches of haggard trees and shrubs
That wails, sensing his coming?

Come the night storm his pastoral dream
Veers toward nightmare: after a lightning-flash,
Out of the darkness, like illumined smoke, there rises
An after-image of the scared beasts:
That are not sheep now, but horses, ghost horses—
Eyes ablaze, nostrils flared, ghastly unearthly white
Trampling a field of wetness
Stampeding the night's blackness.

A fleshless spirit is the stern conqueror;
Inclement in his triumph he tramples under
The dark, drenched, entangled shrubs
Whose roots are deep in mire.

And ghastly in whatever light should strike
The horses rear
Spurred by the English ghosts my Father's dream.

His dream is obsession. It is all-consuming.

# BIOGRAPHICAL NOTES

DICK DAVIS. Born 1945 in Portsmouth. He was educated at Withernsea Comprehensive School, Yorkshire, and King's College, Cambridge, where he read English. Since graduating in 1966 he has worked as a teacher in Yorkshire, Greece, Italy and Persia. His poems have appeared in the *Spectator* and the *Tri-Quarterly* of Chicago University.

GREVEL LINDOP. Born 1948 in Liverpool. Educated at Liverpool College and at Wadham College, Oxford, where he read English and for a time was co-editor of the magazine *Carcanet*. Currently doing research at Wolfson College, Oxford, into the intellectual background of late-Victorian fiction. A pamphlet of his poems, *Against the Sea*, was published by Carcanet Press in 1969.

ALASDAIR MACLEAN. Born 1926 in Glasgow, son of Highland parents. Left school at fourteen and drifted around, doing various jobs. In 1966 went to Edinburgh University to read English. Graduated in 1970 and is now at Teacher Training College. Wrote poems sporadically from the age of twenty, but did not take it seriously until about seven years ago when he started to read modern poetry. Since then has appeared in various publications, including *Transatlantic Review, Scottish Poetry*. Lives in his native parish, Ardnamurchan, whenever he can.

WES MAGEE. Born Greenock, Scotland, in 1939. Left school at fifteen, and worked as a bank clerk until called up for National Service with the Intelligence Corps. Eventually gravitated to Goldsmiths' College, University of London, and completed teacher training course. Has taught at a junior school in Swindon since leaving college. Commenced writing (bad poems) in a barrack room in West Germany, and read up most prose and poetry written since 1950. Ran a poetry magazine *Prism* while at Goldsmiths' and also organized Arts events and festivals there.

His poems have appeared in the *Spectator*, *Encounter*, *Transatlantic Review*, *Tribune*, etc., and he has read on BBC—Radio 1. A booklet, *Postcard from a Long Way Off*, brought out by Ulsterman Publications, appeared in 1970.


PETE MORGAN. Born 1939 in Leigh, Lancashire. Joined the British Army at the age of eighteen, and resigned his commission in 1963. After various jobs he ended up in public relations, but gave it up in 1969 to live by freelance writing.

Has been writing since he was sixteen, and his work has appeared in several magazines, including *Poetry Review*, *Akros*, *Lines Review* and *Scottish International*. The Kevin Press published two booklets of his poems, *A Big Hat or What* in 1968 and *Loss of Two Anchors* in 1970. He received an Arts Council bursary, also in 1970. Lives in Edinburgh with his wife Kate and two children, and appears regularly at the Festival readings in the Traverse Theatre.


PAUL MULDOON. Born 1951, in County Armagh. Educated at Armagh College, he is now studying English at Queen's University, Belfast. His poems have appeared in magazines and journals in Ireland and England.


WILLIAM PESKETT. Born in Cambridge in 1952 but has lived in Belfast for eleven years. Started writing four years ago but much of his early work lost or gladly forgotten. No regrets about the process of growing up. Poems first published in 1968 in the *London Magazine*. They have appeared in various other publications, including *Dublin Magazine*, *Irish Press* and *Ulster Railings*, and have been broadcast. He's currently studying Natural Sciences at Cambridge.


RICHARD RYAN. Born 11th December 1946. B.A. and M.A. in Anglo-Irish studies from University College, Dublin. First collection, *Ledges*, published by the Dolmen Press, Dublin, in April 1970. Editor since 1967 of an annual broadsheet of poetry published in Dublin. Travels as much as possible; in 1970–71 visiting poet at the College of St. Thomas, St. Paul, Minnesota, after which he returns to Dublin to complete a study of the Irish writer, Liam O'Flaherty.


CLIVE WILMER. Born February 1945 in Harrogate, Yorkshire, but grew up and was educated in South London. Attended Emanuel School, Wandsworth, and later, from 1964 to 1967, King's College, Cambridge. After graduating, taught English for nine months at the British Institute of Florence. Then returned to Cambridge to do research (thesis on Tennyson and Victorian poetry). Has had poems and articles published in various literary magazines including the American journal *The Southern Review*, in a special issue devoted to writing from Britain and the Commonwealth. A pamphlet, *Shade Mariners*, including work by himself and two friends, Dick Davis and Robert Wells, appeared in January 1970.